Obstacles don't have to stop you. If you run into a wall, don't turn around and give up. Figure out how to climb it, go through it, or work around it.

- Michael Jordan

Welcome to **The Recession-Ready Planner**, your trusted companion for confidently navigating through challenging financial times.

Within these pages, you'll find practical tools that will assist you in:

- Crafting a robust budget and tracking your expenses, ensuring every dollar is allocated wisely.
- Setting aside a portion of your income to build savings for your desired goals.
- Building a secure emergency fund to weather unforeseen circumstances, offering you peace of mind and a safety net during challenging times.
- Strategically managing debts and setting a path towards financial freedom.
- Harnessing resources and seeking support from local communities tapping into networks that provide valuable information and financial aid.
- Identifying opportunities amidst adversity that will contribute towards long term wealth.

BUDGETING

Monthly Budget

MONTH:

INCOME

Date	Source	Amount
Total:		

Notes

FIXED EXPENSES

Date	Source	Amount
Total:		

VARIABLE EXPENSES

Date	Source	Amount
Total:		

DEBTS

Date	Source	Amount
Total:		

SUMMARY

Source	Amount
(+) Income	
(–) Fixed expenses	
(–) Variable expenses	
(–) Debts	
Total:	

Monthly Budget

MONTH:

INCOME

Date	Source	Amount
Total:		

Notes

FIXED EXPENSES

Date	Source	Amount
Total:		

VARIABLE EXPENSES

Date	Source	Amount
Total:		

DEBTS

Date	Source	Amount
Total:		

SUMMARY

Source	Amount
(+) Income	
(−) Fixed expenses	
(−) Variable expenses	
(−) Debts	
Total:	

Monthly Budget

MONTH:

INCOME

Date	Source	Amount
Total:		

Notes

FIXED EXPENSES

Date	Source	Amount
Total:		

VARIABLE EXPENSES

Date	Source	Amount
Total:		

DEBTS

Date	Source	Amount
Total:		

SUMMARY

Source	Amount
(+) Income	
(–) Fixed expenses	
(–) Variable expenses	
(–) Debts	
Total:	

Monthly Budget

MONTH:

INCOME

Date	Source	Amount
Total:		

Notes

FIXED EXPENSES

Date	Source	Amount
Total:		

VARIABLE EXPENSES

Date	Source	Amount
Total:		

DEBTS

Date	Source	Amount
Total:		

SUMMARY

Source	Amount
(+) Income	
(-) Fixed expenses	
(-) Variable expenses	
(-) Debts	
Total:	

Monthly Budget

MONTH:

INCOME

Date	Source	Amount
Total:		

Notes

FIXED EXPENSES

Date	Source	Amount
Total:		

VARIABLE EXPENSES

Date	Source	Amount
Total:		

DEBTS

Date	Source	Amount
Total:		

SUMMARY

Source	Amount
(+) Income	
(–) Fixed expenses	
(–) Variable expenses	
(–) Debts	
Total:	

Monthly Budget

MONTH:

INCOME

Date	Source	Amount
Total:		

Notes

FIXED EXPENSES

Date	Source	Amount
Total:		

VARIABLE EXPENSES

Date	Source	Amount
Total:		

DEBTS

Date	Source	Amount
Total:		

SUMMARY

Source	Amount
(+) Income	
(–) Fixed expenses	
(–) Variable expenses	
(–) Debts	
Total:	

Monthly Budget

MONTH:

INCOME

Date	Source	Amount
Total:		

Notes

FIXED EXPENSES

Date	Source	Amount
Total:		

VARIABLE EXPENSES

Date	Source	Amount
Total:		

DEBTS

Date	Source	Amount
Total:		

SUMMARY

Source	Amount
(+) Income	
(–) Fixed expenses	
(–) Variable expenses	
(–) Debts	
Total:	

Monthly Budget

MONTH:

INCOME

Date	Source	Amount
Total:		

Notes

FIXED EXPENSES

Date	Source	Amount
Total:		

VARIABLE EXPENSES

Date	Source	Amount
Total:		

DEBTS

Date	Source	Amount
Total:		

SUMMARY

Source	Amount
(+) Income	
(–) Fixed expenses	
(–) Variable expenses	
(–) Debts	
Total:	

Monthly Budget

MONTH:

INCOME

Date	Source	Amount
Total:		

Notes

FIXED EXPENSES

Date	Source	Amount
Total:		

VARIABLE EXPENSES

Date	Source	Amount
Total:		

DEBTS

Date	Source	Amount
Total:		

SUMMARY

Source	Amount
(+) Income	
(−) Fixed expenses	
(−) Variable expenses	
(−) Debts	
Total:	

Monthly Budget

MONTH:

INCOME

Date	Source	Amount
Total:		

Notes

FIXED EXPENSES

Date	Source	Amount
Total:		

VARIABLE EXPENSES

Date	Source	Amount
Total:		

DEBTS

Date	Source	Amount
Total:		

SUMMARY

Source	Amount
(+) Income	
(−) Fixed expenses	
(−) Variable expenses	
(−) Debts	
Total:	

Monthly Budget

MONTH:

INCOME

Date	Source	Amount
Total:		

Notes

FIXED EXPENSES

Date	Source	Amount
Total:		

VARIABLE EXPENSES

Date	Source	Amount
Total:		

DEBTS

Date	Source	Amount
Total:		

SUMMARY

Source	Amount
(+) Income	
(–) Fixed expenses	
(–) Variable expenses	
(–) Debts	
Total:	

Monthly Budget

MONTH:

INCOME

Date	Source	Amount
Total:		

Notes

FIXED EXPENSES

Date	Source	Amount
Total:		

VARIABLE EXPENSES

Date	Source	Amount
Total:		

DEBTS

Date	Source	Amount
Total:		

SUMMARY

Source	Amount
(+) Income	
(–) Fixed expenses	
(–) Variable expenses	
(–) Debts	
Total:	

Monthly Budget

MONTH:

INCOME

Date	Source	Amount
Total:		

Notes

FIXED EXPENSES

Date	Source	Amount
Total:		

VARIABLE EXPENSES

Date	Source	Amount
Total:		

DEBTS

Date	Source	Amount
Total:		

SUMMARY

Source	Amount
(+) Income	
(−) Fixed expenses	
(−) Variable expenses	
(−) Debts	
Total:	

Monthly Budget

MONTH:

INCOME

Date	Source	Amount
Total:		

Notes

FIXED EXPENSES

Date	Source	Amount
Total:		

VARIABLE EXPENSES

Date	Source	Amount
Total:		

DEBTS

Date	Source	Amount
Total:		

SUMMARY

Source	Amount
(+) Income	
(–) Fixed expenses	
(–) Variable expenses	
(–) Debts	
Total:	

Monthly Budget

MONTH:

INCOME

Date	Source	Amount
Total:		

Notes

FIXED EXPENSES

Date	Source	Amount
Total:		

VARIABLE EXPENSES

Date	Source	Amount
Total:		

DEBTS

Date	Source	Amount
Total:		

SUMMARY

Source	Amount
(+) Income	
(–) Fixed expenses	
(–) Variable expenses	
(–) Debts	
Total:	

Monthly Budget

MONTH:

INCOME

Date	Source	Amount
Total:		

Notes

FIXED EXPENSES

Date	Source	Amount
Total:		

VARIABLE EXPENSES

Date	Source	Amount
Total:		

DEBTS

Date	Source	Amount
Total:		

SUMMARY

Source	Amount
(+) Income	
(−) Fixed expenses	
(−) Variable expenses	
(−) Debts	
Total:	

Monthly Budget

MONTH:

INCOME

Date	Source	Amount
Total:		

Notes

FIXED EXPENSES

Date	Source	Amount
Total:		

VARIABLE EXPENSES

Date	Source	Amount
Total:		

DEBTS

Date	Source	Amount
Total:		

SUMMARY

Source	Amount
(+) Income	
(–) Fixed expenses	
(–) Variable expenses	
(–) Debts	
Total:	

Monthly Budget

MONTH:

INCOME

Date	Source	Amount
Total:		

Notes

FIXED EXPENSES

Date	Source	Amount
Total:		

VARIABLE EXPENSES

Date	Source	Amount
Total:		

DEBTS

Date	Source	Amount
Total:		

SUMMARY

Source	Amount
(+) Income	
(−) Fixed expenses	
(−) Variable expenses	
(−) Debts	
Total:	

Monthly Budget

MONTH:

INCOME

Date	Source	Amount
Total:		

Notes

FIXED EXPENSES

Date	Source	Amount
Total:		

VARIABLE EXPENSES

Date	Source	Amount
Total:		

DEBTS

Date	Source	Amount
Total:		

SUMMARY

Source	Amount
(+) Income	
(-) Fixed expenses	
(-) Variable expenses	
(-) Debts	
Total:	

SAVINGS

Savings Milestones

DATE:	MILESTONE :
DATE:	MILESTONE :
DATE:	MILESTONE :
DATE:	MILESTONE :
DATE:	MILESTONE :
DATE:	MILESTONE :
DATE:1	MILESTONE :
DATE:	MILESTONE :

Savings Milestones

DATE:	MILESTONE :
DATE:	MILESTONE :
DATE:	MILESTONE :
DATE:	MILESTONE :
DATE:	MILESTONE :
DATE:	MILESTONE :
DATE:1	MILESTONE :
DATE:	MILESTONE :

Savings

Saving For : ____________________

Date : ____________________

Target Date : ____________________

SUMMARY

Week/Month	Goal	Actual	Remaining	Notes
	TOTAL :			

Savings

Saving For : ______________________

Date : ______________________

Target Date : ______________________

SUMMARY

Week/Month	Goal	Actual	Remaining	Notes
	TOTAL :			

Savings

Saving For : ______________________

Date : ______________________

Target Date : ______________________

SUMMARY

Week/Month	Goal	Actual	Remaining	Notes

TOTAL :

Savings

Saving For : ______________________

Date : ______________________

Target Date : ______________________

SUMMARY

Week/Month	Goal	Actual	Remaining	Notes

TOTAL :

Savings

Saving For : ______________________

Date : ______________________

Target Date : ______________________

SUMMARY

Week/Month	Goal	Actual	Remaining	Notes
	TOTAL :			

Savings

Saving For : ____________________

Date : ____________________

Target Date : ____________________

SUMMARY

Week/Month	Goal	Actual	Remaining	Notes
	TOTAL :			

Savings

Saving For : ______________________

Date : ______________________

Target Date : ______________________

SUMMARY

Week/Month	Goal	Actual	Remaining	Notes

TOTAL :

Savings

Saving For : ______________________

Date : ______________________

Target Date : ______________________

SUMMARY

Week/Month	Goal	Actual	Remaining	Notes
	TOTAL :			

Savings

Saving For : ______________________

Date : ______________________

Target Date : ______________________

SUMMARY

Week/Month	Goal	Actual	Remaining	Notes
	TOTAL :			

Savings

Saving For : ______________________

Date : ______________________

Target Date : ______________________

SUMMARY

Week/Month	Goal	Actual	Remaining	Notes
	TOTAL :			

Savings

Saving For : ______________________

Date : ______________________

Target Date : ______________________

SUMMARY

Week/Month	Goal	Actual	Remaining	Notes

TOTAL :

Savings

Saving For : ______________________

Date : ______________________

Target Date : ______________________

SUMMARY

Week/Month	Goal	Actual	Remaining	Notes

TOTAL :

Savings

Saving For : ______________________

Date : ______________________

Target Date : ______________________

SUMMARY

Week/Month	Goal	Actual	Remaining	Notes

TOTAL :

EMERGENCY FUND

Emergency Funds Planner

Goals	Motivation

Starting Balance:

Required Funds:

Weekly Target:

Monthly Target:

Due Date:

Notes

Funds Tracker

MONTH:

YEAR:

DATE	MEMO	WITHDRAWAL	DEPOSIT	BALANCE

Funds Tracker

MONTH:

YEAR:

DATE	MEMO	WITHDRAWAL	DEPOSIT	BALANCE

Funds Tracker

MONTH:

YEAR:

DATE	MEMO	WITHDRAWAL	DEPOSIT	BALANCE

Funds Tracker

MONTH: | YEAR:

DATE	MEMO	WITHDRAWAL	DEPOSIT	BALANCE

DEBT MANAGEMENT

Debt Payment Tracker

CREDITOR:		
ACCOUNT NO:		
INTEREST RATE:		
STARTING BALANCE:		
DUE DATE:		
MONTH	PAID	BALANCE
JAN		
FEB		
MAR		
APR		
MAY		
JUN		
JUL		
AUG		
SEP		
OCT		
NOV		
DEC		

CREDITOR:		
ACCOUNT NO:		
INTEREST RATE:		
STARTING BALANCE:		
DUE DATE:		
MONTH	PAID	BALANCE
JAN		
FEB		
MAR		
APR		
MAY		
JUN		
JUL		
AUG		
SEP		
OCT		
NOV		
DEC		

CREDITOR:		
ACCOUNT NO:		
INTEREST RATE:		
STARTING BALANCE:		
DUE DATE:		
MONTH	PAID	BALANCE
JAN		
FEB		
MAR		
APR		
MAY		
JUN		
JUL		
AUG		
SEP		
OCT		
NOV		
DEC		

CREDITOR:		
ACCOUNT NO:		
INTEREST RATE:		
STARTING BALANCE:		
DUE DATE:		
MONTH	PAID	BALANCE
JAN		
FEB		
MAR		
APR		
MAY		
JUN		
JUL		
AUG		
SEP		
OCT		
NOV		
DEC		

Debt Payment Tracker

CREDITOR:		
ACCOUNT NO:		
INTEREST RATE:		
STARTING BALANCE:		
DUE DATE:		
MONTH	PAID	BALANCE
JAN		
FEB		
MAR		
APR		
MAY		
JUN		
JUL		
AUG		
SEP		
OCT		
NOV		
DEC		

CREDITOR:		
ACCOUNT NO:		
INTEREST RATE:		
STARTING BALANCE:		
DUE DATE:		
MONTH	PAID	BALANCE
JAN		
FEB		
MAR		
APR		
MAY		
JUN		
JUL		
AUG		
SEP		
OCT		
NOV		
DEC		

CREDITOR:		
ACCOUNT NO:		
INTEREST RATE:		
STARTING BALANCE:		
DUE DATE:		
MONTH	PAID	BALANCE
JAN		
FEB		
MAR		
APR		
MAY		
JUN		
JUL		
AUG		
SEP		
OCT		
NOV		
DEC		

CREDITOR:		
ACCOUNT NO:		
INTEREST RATE:		
STARTING BALANCE:		
DUE DATE:		
MONTH	PAID	BALANCE
JAN		
FEB		
MAR		
APR		
MAY		
JUN		
JUL		
AUG		
SEP		
OCT		
NOV		
DEC		

Debt Payment Tracker

CREDITOR:		
ACCOUNT NO:		
INTEREST RATE:		
STARTING BALANCE:		
DUE DATE:		

MONTH	PAID	BALANCE
JAN		
FEB		
MAR		
APR		
MAY		
JUN		
JUL		
AUG		
SEP		
OCT		
NOV		
DEC		

CREDITOR:		
ACCOUNT NO:		
INTEREST RATE:		
STARTING BALANCE:		
DUE DATE:		

MONTH	PAID	BALANCE
JAN		
FEB		
MAR		
APR		
MAY		
JUN		
JUL		
AUG		
SEP		
OCT		
NOV		
DEC		

CREDITOR:		
ACCOUNT NO:		
INTEREST RATE:		
STARTING BALANCE:		
DUE DATE:		

MONTH	PAID	BALANCE
JAN		
FEB		
MAR		
APR		
MAY		
JUN		
JUL		
AUG		
SEP		
OCT		
NOV		
DEC		

CREDITOR:		
ACCOUNT NO:		
INTEREST RATE:		
STARTING BALANCE:		
DUE DATE:		

MONTH	PAID	BALANCE
JAN		
FEB		
MAR		
APR		
MAY		
JUN		
JUL		
AUG		
SEP		
OCT		
NOV		
DEC		

Debt Snowball Tracker

MONTH OF

CREDITOR

ACCOUNT #

DATE

DUE DATE

INTEREST RATE

GOAL PAYOFF DATE

MINIMUM PAYMENT

DATE	ACCOUNT	BALANCE	NOTES

VISUAL PAYOFF PROGRESS

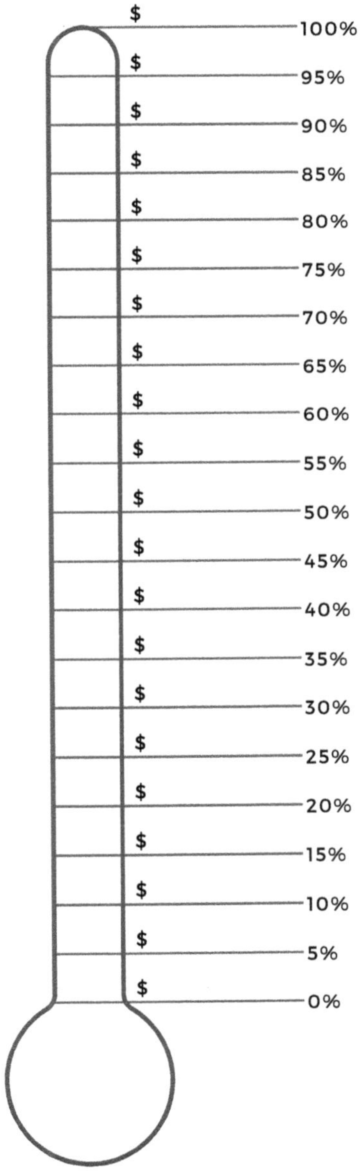

Debt Snowball Tracker

MONTH OF

CREDITOR

ACCOUNT #

DATE

DUE DATE

INTEREST RATE

GOAL PAYOFF DATE

MINIMUM PAYMENT

DATE	ACCOUNT	BALANCE	NOTES

VISUAL PAYOFF PROGRESS

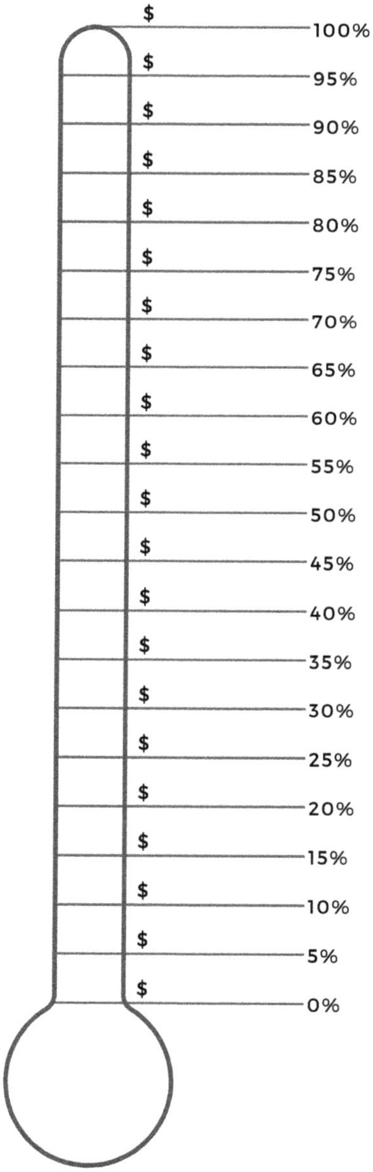

Debt Snowball Tracker

MONTH OF

CREDITOR

ACCOUNT #

DATE

DUE DATE

INTEREST RATE

GOAL PAYOFF DATE

MINIMUM PAYMENT

DATE	ACCOUNT	BALANCE	NOTES

VISUAL PAYOFF PROGRESS

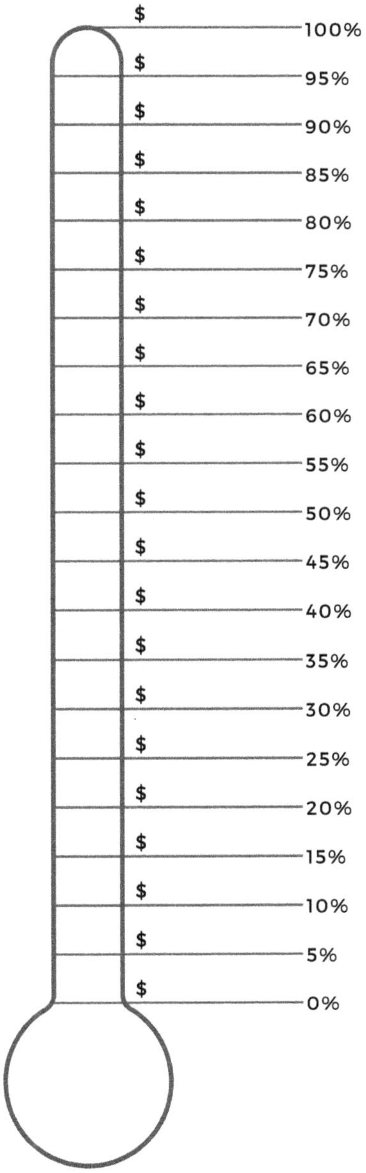

Debt Snowball Tracker

MONTH OF

CREDITOR

ACCOUNT #

DATE

DUE DATE

INTEREST RATE

GOAL PAYOFF DATE

MINIMUM PAYMENT

DATE	ACCOUNT	BALANCE	NOTES

VISUAL PAYOFF PROGRESS

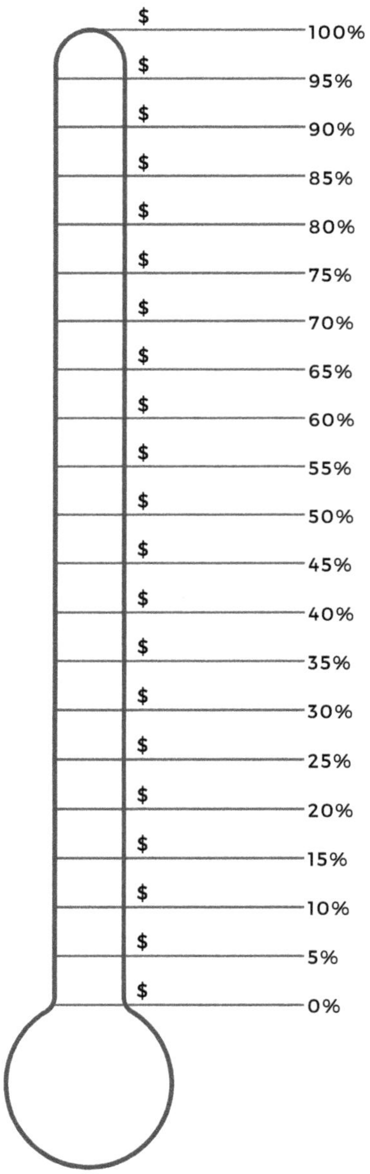

Debt Snowball Tracker

MONTH OF

CREDITOR

ACCOUNT #

DATE

DUE DATE

INTEREST RATE

GOAL PAYOFF DATE

MINIMUM PAYMENT

DATE	ACCOUNT	BALANCE	NOTES

VISUAL PAYOFF PROGRESS

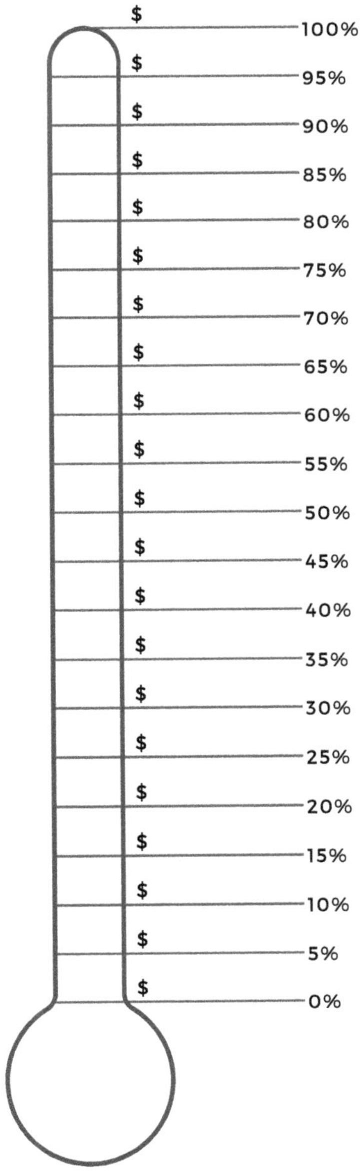

Debt Snowball Tracker

MONTH OF

CREDITOR

ACCOUNT #

DATE

DUE DATE

INTEREST RATE

GOAL PAYOFF DATE

MINIMUM PAYMENT

DATE	ACCOUNT	BALANCE	NOTES

VISUAL PAYOFF PROGRESS

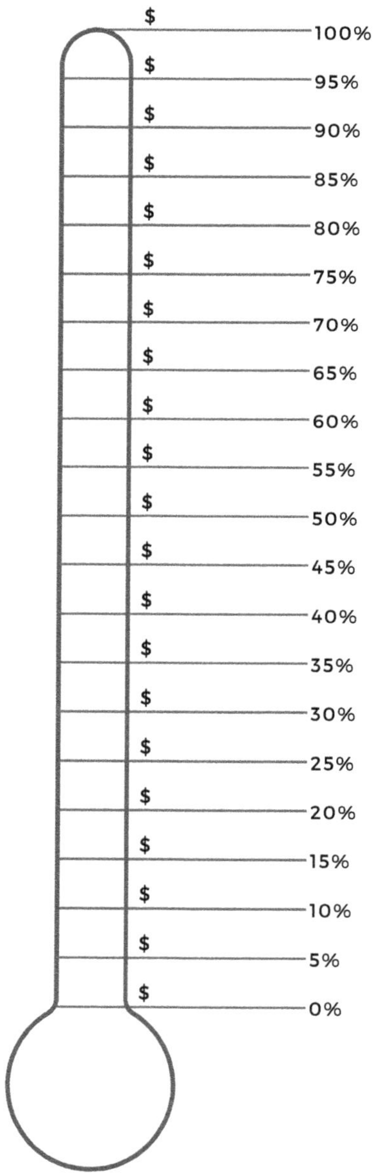

Debt Snowball Tracker

MONTH OF

CREDITOR

ACCOUNT #

DATE

DUE DATE

INTEREST RATE

GOAL PAYOFF DATE

MINIMUM PAYMENT

DATE	ACCOUNT	BALANCE	NOTES

VISUAL PAYOFF PROGRESS

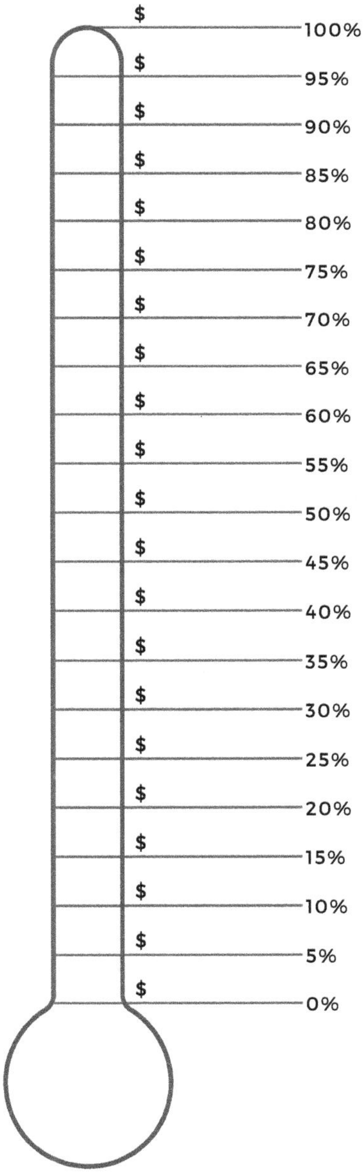

Debt Snowball Tracker

MONTH OF

CREDITOR

ACCOUNT #

DATE

DUE DATE

INTEREST RATE

GOAL PAYOFF DATE

MINIMUM PAYMENT

DATE	ACCOUNT	BALANCE	NOTES

VISUAL PAYOFF PROGRESS

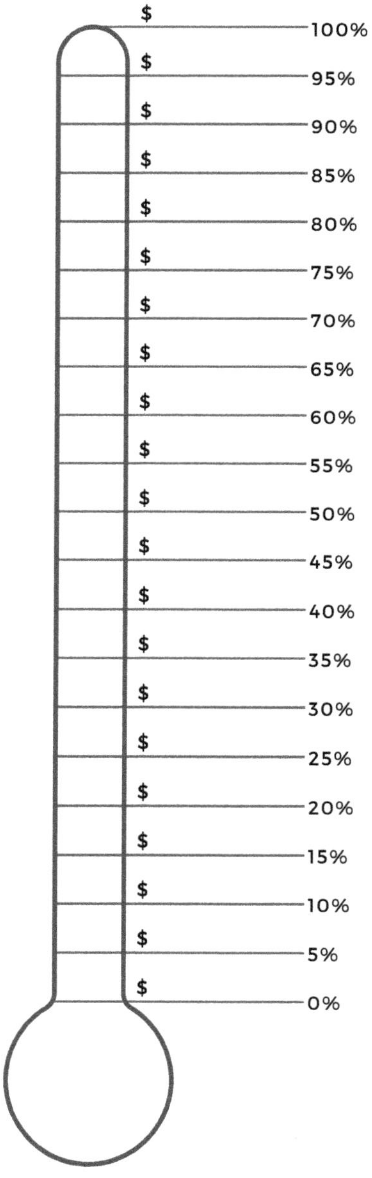

Debt Snowball Tracker

MONTH OF

CREDITOR | ACCOUNT #

DATE | DUE DATE | INTEREST RATE

GOAL PAYOFF DATE | MINIMUM PAYMENT

DATE	ACCOUNT	BALANCE	NOTES

VISUAL PAYOFF PROGRESS

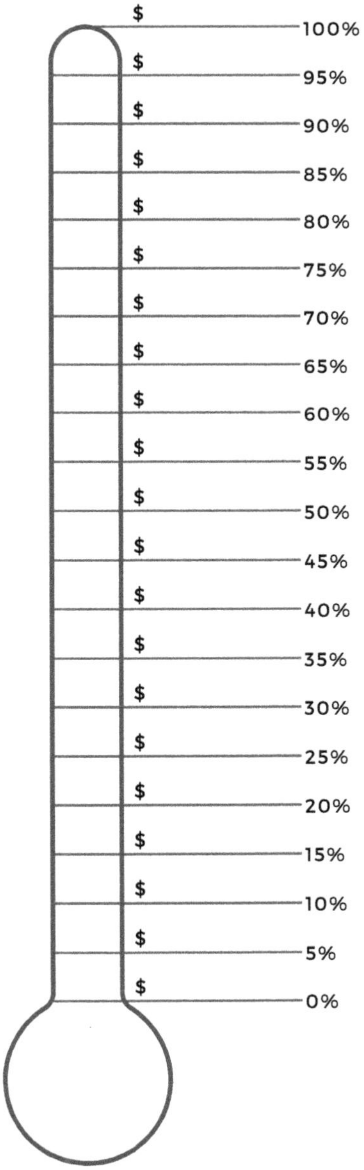

Debt Snowball Tracker

MONTH OF

CREDITOR

ACCOUNT #

DATE

DUE DATE

INTEREST RATE

GOAL PAYOFF DATE

MINIMUM PAYMENT

DATE	ACCOUNT	BALANCE	NOTES

VISUAL PAYOFF PROGRESS

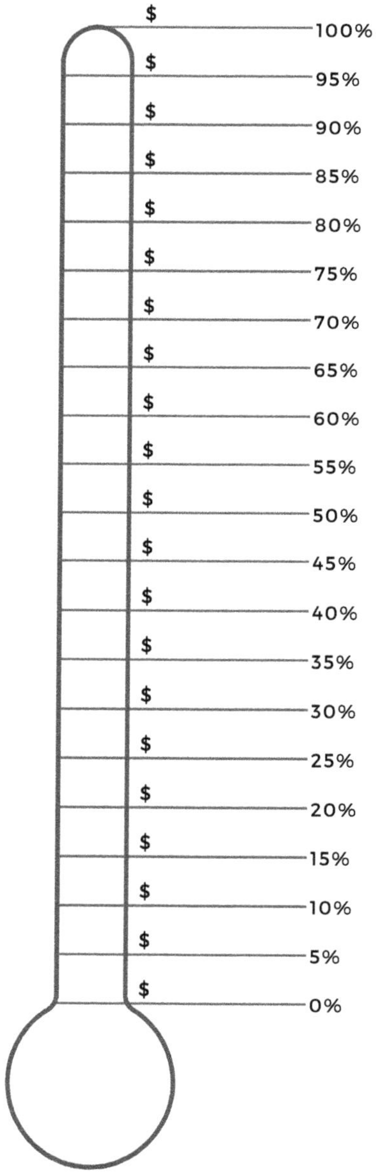

Debt Snowball Tracker

MONTH OF

CREDITOR

ACCOUNT #

DATE

DUE DATE

INTEREST RATE

GOAL PAYOFF DATE

MINIMUM PAYMENT

DATE	ACCOUNT	BALANCE	NOTES

VISUAL PAYOFF PROGRESS

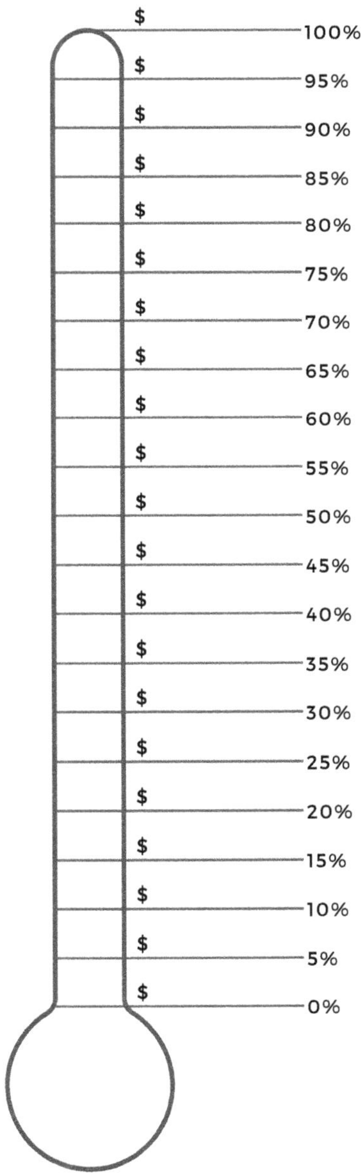

Debt Snowball Tracker

MONTH OF

CREDITOR | ACCOUNT #

DATE | DUE DATE | INTEREST RATE

GOAL PAYOFF DATE | MINIMUM PAYMENT

DATE	ACCOUNT	BALANCE	NOTES

VISUAL PAYOFF PROGRESS

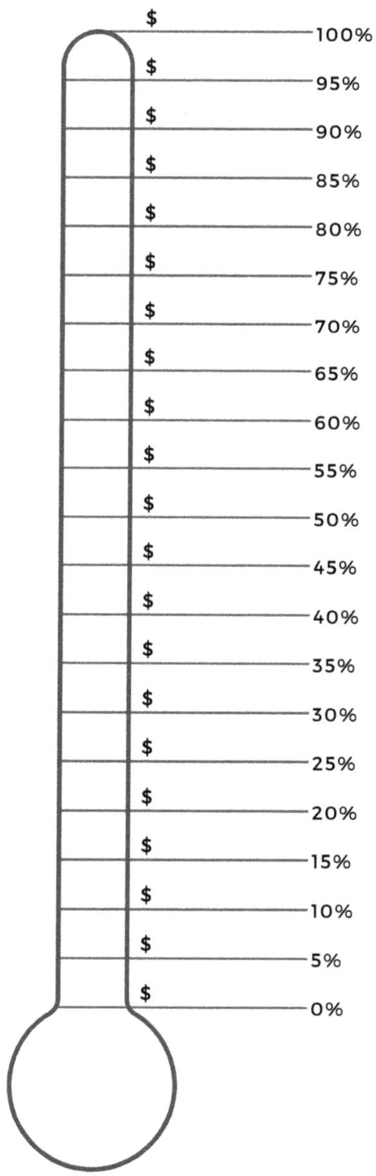

RESOURCES

Assets

Asset Name	Description	Liq. Value on date: ___/___	Liq. Value on date: ___/___	Liq. Value on date: ___/___	Liq. Value on date: ___/___

Assets

Asset Name	Description	Liq. Value on date: ___/___	Liq. Value on date: ___/___	Liq. Value on date: ___/___	Liq. Value on date: ___/___

Assets

Asset Name	Description	Liq. Value on date: ___/___	Liq. Value on date: ___/___	Liq. Value on date: ___/___	Liq. Value on date: ___/___

Assets

Asset Name	Description	Liq. Value on date: ___/___	Liq. Value on date: ___/___	Liq. Value on date: ___/___	Liq. Value on date: ___/___

Assets

Asset Name	Description	Liq. Value on date: ___/___	Liq. Value on date: ___/___	Liq. Value on date: ___/___	Liq. Value on date: ___/___

Assets

Asset Name	Description	Liq. Value on date: ___/___	Liq. Value on date: ___/___	Liq. Value on date: ___/___	Liq. Value on date: ___/___

Friends Family & Acquaintances

Name	Relationship	Contact Information	Notes

Friends Family & Acquaintances

Name	Relationship	Contact Information	Notes

Friends Family & Acquaintances

Name	Relationship	Contact Information	Notes

Friends Family & Acquaintances

Name	Relationship	Contact Information	Notes

Friends Family & Acquaintances

Name	Relationship	Contact Information	Notes

Financial Assistance Programs

Program Name	Description	Elegibility Requirements	Contact Information

Financial Assistance Programs

Program Name	Description	Elegibility Requirements	Contact Information

Legal Aid Services

Service Provider Name	Areas of Legal Aid	Contact Information	Fees

Legal Aid Services

Service Provider Name	Areas of Legal Aid	Contact Information	Fees

Government Resources

Resource Name	Description	Contact Information	Notes

Government Resources

Resource Name	Description	Contact Information	Notes

Financial Counseling Services

Service Provider Name	Areas of Expertise	Contact Information	Fees

Financial Counseling Services

Service Provider Name	Areas of Expertise	Contact Information	Fees

OPPORTUNITIES

Stock Market Opportunities

Stock Ticker/ Company Name	Target Investment	Target Price	Risk Level & Investment Timeline	Research Notes

Stock Market Opportunities

Stock Ticker/ Company Name	Target Investment	Target Price	Risk Level & Investment Timeline	Research Notes

Stock Market Opportunities

Stock Ticker/ Company Name	Target Investment	Target Price	Risk Level & Investment Timeline	Research Notes

Stock Market Opportunities

Stock Ticker/ Company Name	Target Investment	Target Price	Risk Level & Investment Timeline	Research Notes

Stock Market Opportunities

Stock Ticker/ Company Name	Target Investment	Target Price	Risk Level & Investment Timeline	Research Notes

Stock Market Opportunities

Stock Ticker/ Company Name	Target Investment	Target Price	Risk Level & Investment Timeline	Research Notes

Other Investment Opportunities

Name	Investment Amount	Risk Level & Investment Timeline	Investment Contacts	Research Notes

Other Investment Opportunities

Name	Investment Amount	Risk Level & Investment Timeline	Investment Contacts	Research Notes

Other Investment Opportunities

Name	Investment Amount	Risk Level & Investment Timeline	Investment Contacts	Research Notes

Other Investment Opportunities

Name	Investment Amount	Risk Level & Investment Timeline	Investment Contacts	Research Notes

Professional Development

Program Name	Provider	Dates	Skills / Certifications

Professional Development

Program Name	Provider	Dates	Skills / Certifications

Job Market Research

Industry	Positions	Requirements	Companies

Job Market Research

Industry	Positions	Requirements	Companies

Side Hustle Ideas

Idea Description	Potential Market/ Demand	Startup Costs	Action Steps

Side Hustle Ideas

Idea Description	Potential Market/ Demand	Startup Costs	Action Steps

Entrepreneurial Ventures

Venture Idea	Market Analysis	Resources Needed	Milestones

Entrepreneurial Ventures

Venture Idea	Market Analysis	Resources Needed	Milestones

Networking Events

Event Name	Date, Time & Location	Key Speakers	Contacts Made/Insights Gained

Networking Events

Event Name	Date, Time & Location	Key Speakers	Contacts Made/Insights Gained

NOTES

NOTES

NOTES

NOTES

NOTES

NOTES

NOTES

www.ingramcontent.com/pod-product-compliance
Lightning Source LLC
Chambersburg PA
CBHW041255150926
51501CB00011B/208
9781962173001